D0970527

RULES *for* MY
DAUGHTER

Let's get some things straight
before I get old and uncool.

RULES *for* MY DAUGHTER

Walker Lamond

Atlantic Books
London

First published as *Rules for My Newborn Daughter* in the United States in 2016 by St Martin's Press, an imprint of Macmillan Publishers.

First published in Great Britain in 2016 by Atlantic Books, an imprint of Atlantic Books Ltd.

10 9 8 7 6 5 4 3 2 1

A CIP catalogue record for this book is available from the British Library.

Hardback ISBN: 978 1 78649 0 117
E-book ISBN: 978 1 78649 0 124

Printed in Italy by Grafica Veneta S.p.A.

Atlantic Books
An Imprint of Atlantic Books Ltd
Ormond House
26–27 Boswell Street
London
WC1N 3JZ

www.atlantic-books.co.uk

for

FRANCES

Introduction

But what if it's a girl?

That's the question I was asked most frequently after I published my first book, *Rules for My Son*, which I described so self-assuredly as 'one man's instructions for raising a thoughtful, adventurous, honest, hardworking, self-reliant, well-dressed, well-read, well-mannered young gentleman'. Many readers, my wife included, wanted to know whether my unsolicited advice could be applied to girls as well as boys.

My answer, of course, was ... of course! While the book, and the blog from which it sprung, was imagined as a decidedly one-sided conversation between father and son, I was confident that just about every rule could be applied to a future daughter as well as my then-unborn son. After all, writing thank-you notes, keeping a tidy lawn, and learning how to shake a martini are universal lessons and hardly the exclusive realm of men. But then again, there were all those rules about dating girls. And tying a necktie. And a few dozen other rules that were admittedly pretty male-centric, if not explicitly, then at least in tone. My wife thought that our future daughter deserved her own rules. Maybe even a whole book of them. I agreed.

Boys and girls are equally capable and equally thirsty for all the institutional knowledge that a parent can muster. But they are also different. Wonderfully, obviously, and sometimes hilariously different. And never was this more obvious than when shortly after I finished *Rules for My Son* my wife and I had our second child – a girl.

So I decided to write a book for her too. But I did have a nagging concern. In this day and age, was it appropriate for a man to be doling out advice to a young woman? What did I know about the unique challenges of being a girl? And if I wanted my daughter to grow into a strong, independent, brave young woman who was unafraid to challenge traditional power structures and antiquated gender stereotypes, was handing her a book full of rules written by a man best way to start her journey?

The answer is … I don't know. I am no parenting expert. I'm just a dad. And I think a dad has a right and a duty to tell his daughter what he expects of her. To share with her what he knows about life and how to make the best of it. And while I might not know even a fraction of what it takes to become an independent, intelligent, courteous, courageous, honest, adventurous, self-reliant, well-read, well-dressed, well-mannered young woman, I do know someone who does. Thankfully, I married her.

WHEN IN DOUBT,
WEAR A DRESS.

EAT LUNCH WITH
THE NEW GIRL.

IF YOU CAN FOLLOW A RECIPE,
YOU CAN BUILD A TABLE.

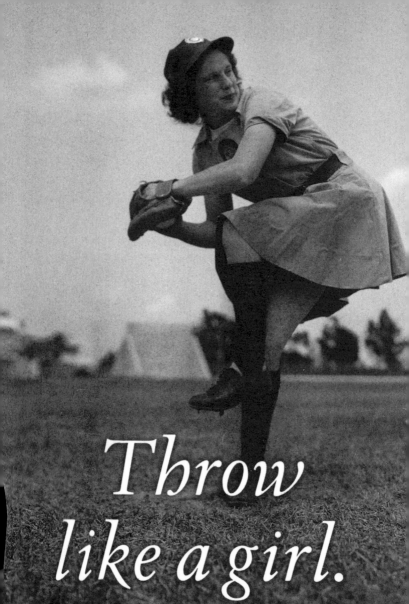

Throw
like a girl.

CLIMB TREES.
Skin knees.

A foreign accent
does not make him
more sophisticated.

Let him take your coat.
That's the moment he's
been waiting for.

Never play dumb.

EXCEPT AT THE POKER TABLE.

TRY NOT TO
MAKE FUN OF YOUR
BROTHER IN FRONT OF
OTHER GIRLS.

The best way to remove
red wine is with white wine.

*If you start the day in
tracksuit bottoms, you will
likely end the day in them.*

Dance with your dad.
And not just on your
wedding day.

There's more to life than being a passenger.

Amelia Earhart

ON A FIRST DATE,

ORDER THE STEAK.

Learn to sew
your own clothes.
You'll become a
better shopper.

Never trust a profile pic.
Not even your own.

The right friends will
appreciate a well-timed burp.
Your grandmother will not.

If the food's not perfect,
DON'T BLAME
the waiter.

**Not everything is a
photo opportunity.**

**NEVER SWITCH A SEATING CARD
AT THE DINNER TABLE.**

*Everybody loves
a high-five.*

I don't care if *Granny* is on *Instagram;* phones down at the table.

✻

There's *nothing cooler* than a girl who can change a tyre.

✻

Remember, it's a speed limit, not a speed minimum.

THERE IS A RIGHT WAY,
AND A VERY *WRONG* WAY
TO EXIT A CAR IN A DRESS.

*When it comes to relationships,
people change their minds.
You can too.*

Writing an essay is easy.
Just think of it as a
hundred tweets.

Practise safe selfies.

NEVER STAND AT
THE EDGES OF A
GROUP PHOTO.
IF THE CROP
DOESN'T GET
YOU, THE WIDE
ANGLE WILL.

Use the good china.
Even for takeaways.

JUST HIRE MOVERS.

NEVER STOP
EXPLORING.

Resist the humblebrag.

Maybe not so many pillows.

YES, YOU CAN ENTER A
BEAUTY CONTEST . . .
AS SOON AS YOU EARN YOUR
ENGINEERING DEGREE.

Tell people exactly
what you want.

Bring bagels.

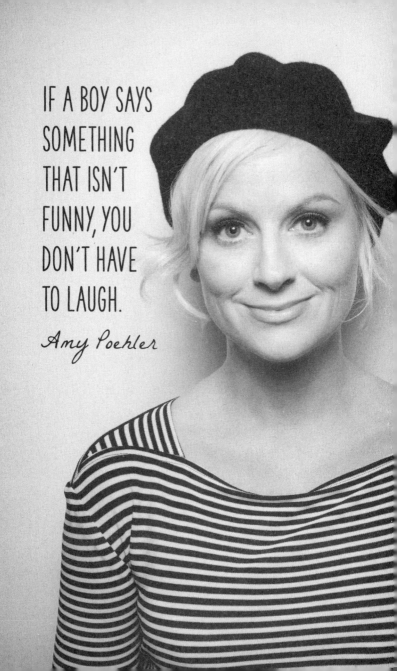

IF A BOY SAYS
SOMETHING
THAT ISN'T
FUNNY, YOU
DON'T HAVE
TO LAUGH.

Amy Poehler

You can take a whole doughnut
or no doughnut. Those are
your only options.

If you make a habit of apologizing for other people, it's you who will be sorry.

Resist the temptation to look in every mirror.

A citizen's noblest quality is not patriotism, it's participation.

If you're not crazy about your dance partner, find a friend and triangulate.

We see you checking your phone.

Entertain
at home.

---

*If a guest brings
wine, serve it.*

Never let him win.

Take your dad shopping.

SWEAR INFREQUENTLY.
BUT WHEN YOU DO,
MAKE IT COUNT.

Support a good cause.
But not just for the parties.

⌇

INTRODUCE YOURSELF.

It isn't where you came from, it's where you're going that counts.

Ella Fitzgerald

YOU CANNOT PRETEND
TO BE FAMOUS.

EVERYONE'S BUSY.
NOBODY CARES.

Compliment
your friends
behind their backs.

*Put your camera
away and enjoy
the moment.*

I WILL ALWAYS SING 'HAPPY BIRTHDAY'. IT WILL ALWAYS BE EMBARRASSING.

*You're never too old to
be tucked into bed.*

Make an entrance.
Leave quietly.

Always keep champagne in the fridge and ice cream in the freezer. For emergencies.

You will regret
not dancing.

⟿

As you get older,
my hearing will get worse,
but your mother's will
only get better.

There is no need to sacrifice punctuality for personality.

Sand the wood before you paint.

If you're cool,
you don't have
to prove it.

Always carry
a book.

It's okay to
make him wait.

PLAY THE DRUMS.

Let him lead.
But watch your toes.

YOU'LL NEVER SHOCK ME
WITH YOUR MUSIC.
BUT YOU CAN EDUCATE ME.

Beauty is mostly attitude.
The rest is good lighting.

If the host
suggests charades,
you're playing
charades.

IF SOMETHING IS THAT
MEANINGFUL, YOU SHOULDN'T
NEED A TATTOO TO REMIND YOU.

If the invitation says
wear a costume,
wear a costume.

If you are going to Magaluf, you'd better have a really good reason.

I will never tell you whom to love. But I reserve the right to show him or her pictures of you from middle school.

LEARN
TO
SURF.

I also have a pretty good right hook.

Julie Andrews

Find your range. Not every
girl sings like Julie Andrews.

✼

*Take it easy
on your mother.*

✼

Yes, you can be
too rich and too thin.

*Seriously,
no wire hangers.*

❀

GET
MUDDY.

You can
always squeeze
one more in
for dinner.

*The most meaningful
charity is anonymous.*

YES, I'M
WAITING UP
UNTIL YOU GET
HOME.

Stay up LATE.

LIVE IN PARIS.

Under no circumstances should you ask someone to remove their shoes.

Take the train.

Tell your
MOTHER
you like her
NEW HAIRCUT.

Don't throw away the jam jar.

MONOGRAM WITH ABANDON.

Dance with yourself.
Often.

No one really wants to hear about your diet, your schedule, or what you paid for that dress.

Dads can brush hair too.

Too much good taste
can be boring.

Diana Vreeland

IT'S HARD TO
DRIVE A BARGAIN
CARRYING A DESIGNER HANDBAG.

- - - - - - - - - - - - - - - - - - - -

KNOW WHAT YOU'RE GETTING INTO.
THAT GOES ESPECIALLY
FOR HOT TUBS.

When the
world around you
has nothing more to
offer, by all means,
wear headphones.

~

Accept
with pleasure or
regretfully decline,
but you need not give
a reason why.

Feel free to
straighten his TIE.

IF YOU WANT TO KEEP
FAITH IN THE HUMAN RACE,
DON'T READ THE COMMENTS.

When life gets too busy, bake a pie.

PLANT A GARDEN.

The best cheerleaders
are not on the sidelines,
they're on the field.

Sometimes
ASKING FOR HELP
is the bravest thing
you can do.
Also, stand-up comedy.

The only GOOD
seat in a convertible is
behind the wheel.

LEARN TO IDENTIFY
BIRDS BY SONG, AND
YOU WILL NEVER BE
LONELY AGAIN.

*Time is precious.
Cancel your magazine
subscriptions.*

Don't age gracefully.
Age defiantly.

＊

BEWARE THE LADIES
WHO LUNCH.

A fringe is NOT the answer.

If you need to explain a joke, it probably isn't funny.

Now try it
without the sarcasm.

You can't be friends
with EVERYONE.

*Never cancel dinner
plans by text message.*

REQUEST THE
LATE CHECKOUT.

TAKE HIM TO THE
FOOTBALL.

THE COOLEST KIDS
DON'T EVEN KNOW IT YET.

Don't pawn your grandmother's jewellery.

THE MOST COURAGEOUS
ACT IS STILL TO THINK FOR
YOURSELF. ALOUD.

Coco Chanel

DIET *is not a verb.*

SHARE FAMILY TRADITIONS WITH YOUR PARTNER. BUT LEAVE ROOM FOR NEW ONES.

Don't panic – it's probably just a fuse.

WRITE MORE
LETTERS.

Unless you bought a ticket, *your bag* doesn't get a seat to itself.

A boy has *never* liked a girl for her makeup.

They'll remember the *thank-you note* longer than you'll remember the gift.

No pierced ears until you are sixteen.

Teach him to tie a bow tie.

No one wants to hear
about your family tree.
Usually, not even your
family.

If you are the smartest girl in
your group of friends, maybe
it's time for some new friends.

If you choose
not to own a TV,
keep it to yourself.

When entrusted
with a secret,
KEEP IT.

Watch old movies.
And foreign ones.
And dumb ones.

DON'T GET MARRIED
BEFORE YOU CAN
LEGALLY DRINK.

SUMMER FRIENDS ARE
BEST KEPT IN THE SUMMER.

IF YOU'RE STAYING MORE
THAN ONE NIGHT, UNPACK.

The greatest danger to our future is apathy.

Jane Goodall

You can spare us the photograph of your meal.

Brew your own coffee.

Unless you mean to shout, don't write emails with the Caps Lock on.

If you are blessed with
the ability to wink, use it.

Return a borrowed car
with a **full tank** of petrol.

Never get drunker
than the boss.

There's not a man
on the planet
who hasn't deserved
to have a drink
thrown in his face.

WHEN STIRRING
YOUR TEA,
TRY NOT TO
CLINK THE CUP.

A friend is someone who notices your new haircut.

There's no light more flattering than a campfire.

If he's dancing behind you, you're doing it wrong.

YOU DON'T DRINK WINE AT THE FOOTBALL STADIUM.

If you open someone's gift in front of her, there's no need for a thank-you note.

Too much of a
good thing can be
wonderful.

Mae West

ACCEPTING AN AWARD
IS NO TIME TO
MAKE A SPEECH.

IF YOU LIKE SOMEONE,
ASK HER OUT.

PLAN A FAMILY REUNION.

Keep
your elbows in
and run on
the balls
of your feet.

My coach said I ran like a GIRL. I said if he ran a little faster, he could too.

Mia Hamm

Be mindful of what comes
between you and the earth.
Buy good tyres, good sheets,
and GREAT shoes.

Yoga is not
a competition.

Just because he asked you out, doesn't mean you have to ask him up.

IF YOU COOKED, THEY CLEAN.
AND VICE VERSA.

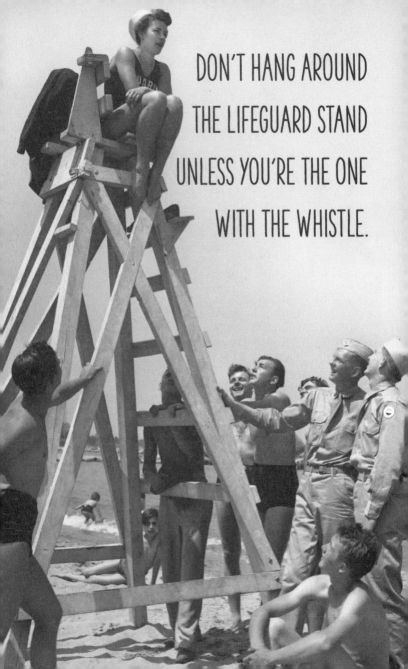

DON'T HANG AROUND
THE LIFEGUARD STAND
UNLESS YOU'RE THE ONE
WITH THE WHISTLE.

Always bring a
housewarming gift.

Don't be the girl with the
most expensive outfit
in the gym.

If a man offers
you his seat,
TAKE IT.

✦

Being a strong
swimmer means
getting your
hair wet.

Never pass up
a water fountain.

If you are driving,
a red light is not an excuse
to check your phone.

If your date *doesn't*
meet you at the door,
don't even bother
opening it.

Pause to appreciate a
well-wrapped gift.

~ꙮꙮꙮꙮ~

Save the ribbons.

Don't apologize for
your opinion before
you've given it.

GROW YOUR OWN
TOMATOES.

Pick wildflowers.

DON'T JUST WATCH
THE BAND. JOIN IT.

Jump on the bed.

Make haste!
You will never be as
young as you are
today.

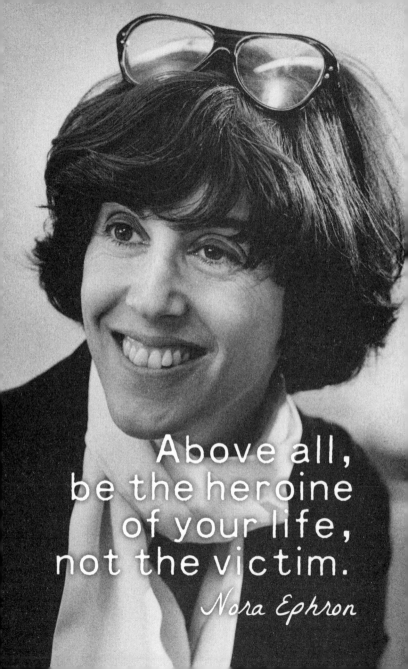

Above all,
be the heroine
of your life,
not the victim.
Nora Ephron

Don't get all your news
from Facebook.

•━◆━•

You can't save all
the animals. But
you can try.

SOMETIMES THE BEST CURE
IS A NIGHT AT YOUR
FAVOURITE HOTEL.

IF YOU HAVE TO MAKE
MORE THAN ONE SUBSTITUTION,
ORDER SOMETHING ELSE.

It's your job to introduce your younger siblings to cool music.

Palm trees make everything better.

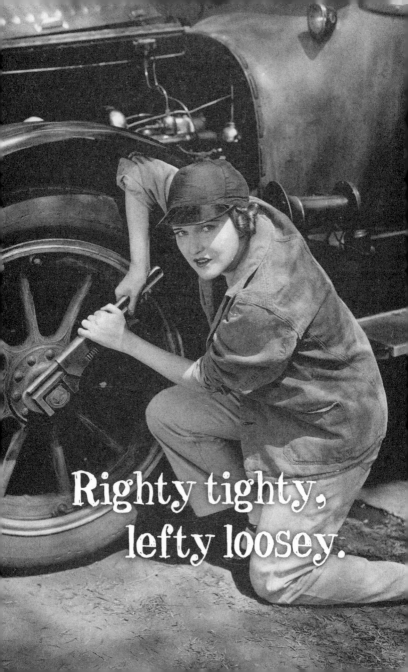

Surprise your mum
at the office.

When meeting people out,
don't suggest the restaurant
closest to your apartment.
Or the most expensive.

Try to lose the adverbs.
Seriously.

Unless you're camping,
feel free to pack
more than you
can carry yourself.

Sometimes the movie is better than the book.

No high heels on a boat.

Don't be afraid of the ball.

Even if your date pays
for dinner, you owe him
nothing in return.
Not even another date.

◆◆◆

*Keep promises.
Especially the ones
to yourself.*

Stand to the right side
of an escalator.
Walk on the left.

———◈———

You can have more than one
BEST FRIEND.

You can't use up creativity. The more you use, the more you have.

Maya Angelou

The airport is not
your bedroom.
Keep your shoes on and
stay off the floor.

Your hair will grow back.
Your eyebrows may not.

GO BAREFOOT.

If you are asked to be a bridesmaid, be the funny one.

You don't have
to listen to him
play guitar.

**SEND POSTCARDS.
YOU CAN'T PUT A TEXT
IN A SHOEBOX.**

Remember
it's the subject
that should do
the posing,
not the artist.

Never turn down free
champagne.

❀

If you're going to reinvent yourself,
at least be original.

IF YOU NEED ADVICE
ON YOUR LOVE LIFE,
ASK YOUR GRANDMOTHER.

NEVER SHOW UP EARLY
TO A DINNER PARTY.

IF YOU THINK YOU DESERVE A RAISE,
ASK FOR ONE.

DON'T WEAR YOUR
HEART ON YOUR
SLEEVE OR
YOUR POLITICS
ON A STICKER.

Buy a used car.

Life is
not measured
in 'likes'.

Here's a rule
I recommend.
Never practise
two vices
at once.

*Tallulah
Bankhead*

In a good
dance routine,
it's NOT the moves
that count, it's the
synchronicity.

• ◆ •

Help Dad clean
out the garage.
He gets sentimental.

The problem with *social climbing* is that the people you look up to will always be *looking down at you.*

Take yourself to dinner.

I'd rather see you
finish a hard task
than master an easy one.

Try not to be
embarrassed
when your parents
cheer for you.
We can't help it.

Return borrowed clothes.
Even your sister's.

You can fix just about
anything in the house
with the right *screwdriver*
and a stepladder.

Backpacking around Europe does
not actually require a backpack.

Applaud with enthusiasm.
But watch the wooing
and the booing.

Don't leave candles
burning when you
leave the room.

If you
cheat on your taxes,
you're a cheater.

*

Don't just store
the silver.

IF AN OUTFIT DOESN'T
FEEL RIGHT, IT PROBABLY ISN'T.

✺

BEWARE OF MEN
WHO CRY EASILY.

✺

GIVEN THE OPPORTUNITY,
USE THE OUTDOOR SHOWER.

NEVER COMPLAIN.
NEVER EXPLAIN.

Katharine Hepburn

The only thing you'll regret more than smoking is all the pictures of you smoking.

The easiest way to express your individualism is through clothes. It's also the least interesting.

Feel free to dye your hair. BUT NOT for your sister's wedding.

~

*Be skeptical.
But always leave room
for a little magic.*

If you really have something to say, better to be behind the camera than in front of it.

There's always time
for a blowout.

*If you're going to look
someone up and down,
it better be followed by
a compliment.*

You can buy your way into the gossip pages, but you can't buy your way out.

If you have the right
of way, take it.

Occasionally,
just order a beer.

If you have a disagreement
with someone, take it offline.

A *diamond* is just a rock.
It's the story behind it
that counts.

Don't eat *less food*.
Eat fewer ingredients.

Avoid drinking alcohol
in a *bikini*.

TAKE GOOD CARE OF YOUR HANDS.

Fruit is like fashion. Always know what's in season.

STAY AWAY
FROM PEOPLE
WHO PUSH
OTHER PEOPLE
INTO POOLS.

If you can't outrun them,
outlast them.

The secret of staying young
is to live honestly, eat slowly,
and lie about your age.

Lucille Ball

You can't tip the postman.
But you can feed him.

CALL YOUR MOTHER.

Don't assign meaning
to the meaningless.
It's exhausting.

No matter where
you are,
I WILL ALWAYS
come get you.

*Try making something
with your own two hands.
Only then can you call
yourself a designer.*

Everyone has a story to tell.
Wait your turn.

The best way to ruin
an apology is with
an explanation.

A road trip is twice as good
with the windows down.

He cares more about his hair than he's letting on.

Your home should give people a glimpse into you, not a catalogue.

IF YOU'RE GOING TO DATE SOMEONE IN THE BAND, DATE THE BASSIST.

No matter what the bride says, you will *never* wear the bridesmaid dress again.

◆

When it comes to
school projects,
presentation is
half the battle.
But only half.

Dress up for the theatre.
Even if you're the only one.

DON'T FALL FOR THE
LEADING MAN.

You don't have to
adopt your boyfriend's
favourite sports team.

Don't do anything that
you can't tell your diary.

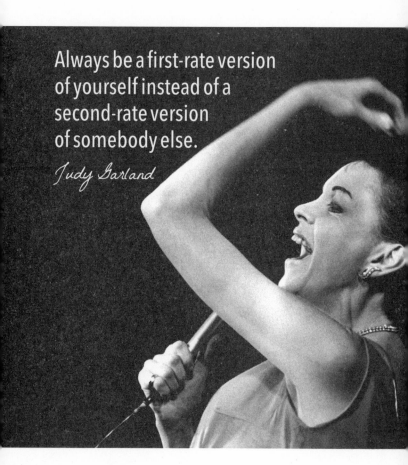

Always be a first-rate version of yourself instead of a second-rate version of somebody else.

Judy Garland

If you really want to
say you're sorry,
bring food.

Sit up straight.

Don't try to *sweet-talk*
the teacher.

GET PLENTY OF SLEEP.
BUT NOT JUST IN THE MORNING.

IF YOU WANT TO TRAVEL THE WORLD,
DEVELOP A TASTE FOR SPICY FOOD.

Let your work speak for itself.

Stay up to watch the sunrise.

If you can still read a magazine, you're not really exercising.

It's not idleness if
you do it in the sun.

Check the
high-tide mark
before you set up
camp.

Sometimes all you
really need is a
home-cooked meal.

□ ———————— □

You don't have to make
money to be an artist.
But it helps.

If you can't *be popular,*
be mysterious.

If you want an *honest*
opinion, ask your aunt.

Don't expect to keep
secrets from the person
who does your laundry.

You can't hope yourself to a better life – you must take yourself there.

Helen Gurley Brown

LAST YEAR'S OUTFIT IS NEXT YEAR'S COSTUME.

✿

Real men do the washing-up.

Your reputation is in the hands of those who know you the least.

•◆•

Keep your eye on the host. She decides how to eat the chicken.

Meet the neighbours.

♦♦♦

Yes, it will look
better with a second
coat of paint.

SOMETIMES GREAT HAIR IS THE BEST REVENGE.

Making cupcakes is cool.
Making a table is cooler.

ALWAYS KEEP
THEM GUESSING.

No, you don't have to
try everything once.

CONSIDER WALLPAPER.

Help a friend win
a girl's heart.

No one's
IMPRESSED
by a car you didn't
BUY YOURSELF.

You are only as nice as you are to strangers.

The moment you lose your temper, you've lost.

Nine times out of ten, you probably aren't having a full-on nervous breakdown – you just need a cup of tea and a biscuit.

Caitlin Moran

Bring a jumper to the cinema.
Especially in the summer.

Unless the situation is dire,
don't hijack the stereo at
someone else's party.

Take a walk in the rain.

Every girl should have
a favourite painting,
poem, and dirty joke.

✦

Don't copy your friend's
new haircut.

✦

*You don't have to smile
in every picture.*

Don't hog the power
socket at a coffee shop.
Even better, don't plug in.

It's 'You're welcome'
not 'No problem'.

Don't be afraid of the rain.
Or mice.

SHARE YOUR
ICE-CREAM CONE.

NEVER KILL A SPIDER.
YOU'LL PAY FOR IT IN
MOSQUITO BITES.

ACCEPT A STUPID BET.

**KEEP YOUR EYES OFF YOUR
PHONE WHEN YOU'RE
CROSSING THE STREET.**

Not every photo needs a filter.

Remember to always thank your hosts.
Once at the door and once by mail.

Get your hands dirty.
But keep your nails clean.

Don't just recycle.
REPAIR,
REPURPOSE,
and REUSE.

There's no such thing as a girl's skateboard.

Make your bed every morning. Good habits are just as hard to break as bad ones.

Sooner or later, you'll regret faking that accent.

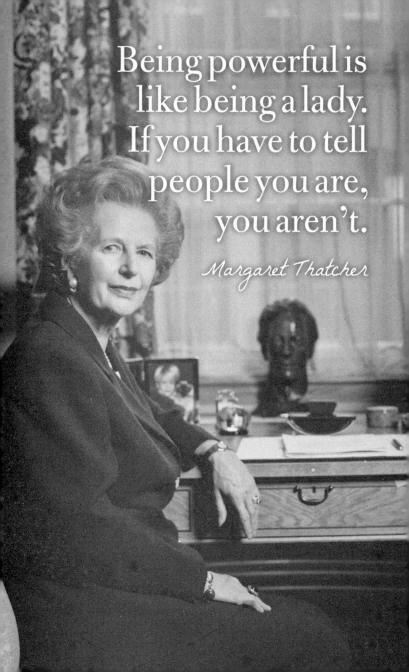

Being powerful is like being a lady. If you have to tell people you are, you aren't.

Margaret Thatcher

Be wary of a man
susceptible to trends.
He can't make up his mind.

When setting a table,
remember that knife
blades face the plate.

**NOT EVERYTHING'S COOLER
IN BLACK AND WHITE.**

A good dinner guest should be prepared to sing for her supper.

Get to know your neighbourhood bookseller.

On occasion, take a holiday from the Internet.

If you can't stand the sand,
stay off the beach.

Learn to take a compliment.

Be optimistic.
Always pack a party dress.

Life is about more than being
happy. It's about making others happy too,
sometimes at a heavy cost to yourself.

If there isn't time for a walk, you're too busy.

At the cinema,
all diets are off.

There's only one way to enter cold water. QUICKLY.

GOSSIP ALWAYS REVEALS MORE ABOUT THE GOSSIPER THAN IT DOES ABOUT THE GOSSIPED.

Don't snoop around in the medicine cabinets.

Never leave the beach without a jump in the ocean.

Hidden gems won't stay hidden forever. *Especially if you brag about them.*

When you're with new friends, resist talking about old friends.

If you chase it, it will run.

IF YOU NEED MUSIC
ON THE BEACH, YOU'RE
MISSING THE POINT.

Never toast to
yourself.

Beware of plans made after last orders.

DON'T BE AFRAID
TO WEAR A FUNNY HAT.
OR A FANCY ONE.

Never request a joke or an impression. They're never as good on command.

Avoid employment at any restaurant that requires a headshot.

Be a reliable babysitter.

THE INTERNET
NEVER FORGETS.

*Eyeglasses may help
you look smart. But fake ones
will only make you
look vain.*

You're never too old to make new friends.

A LITTLE SELF-DEPRECATION
GOES A LONG WAY.

Be yourself. The world
has enough actors.

TRY THE SOUP.

*Don't be afraid to sail
close to the wind.*

Go to church.
If not for the prayer,
for the architecture.

Don't forget that Ginger Rogers
did everything he did
backwards and in high heels.

Bob Thaves

You don't always have to
know where you're going.
Just don't forget
where you've been.

✦

All space and time is an
illusion. You still have to do
your homework.

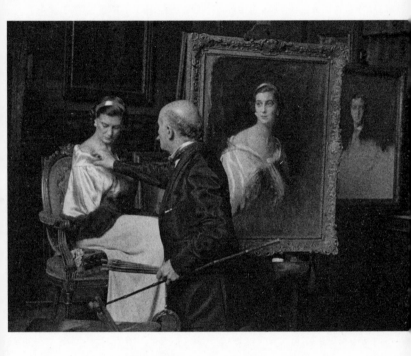

Sit for a portrait.
But never lie down for one.

**SHOPPING
IS** NOT A HOBBY.
IT'S A HABIT.

PRACTICE IS ABOUT
BUILDING UP YOUR
TOLERANCE TO FAILURE.

**VISIT A FRIEND IN
THE HOSPITAL. BRING**
BAD MAGAZINES.

NEVER ask a stranger to
retake a photograph.

Conceiving a child is a choice.
Don't let anyone take it
away from you.

God answers all prayers.
SOMETIMES with a no.

NO TWO SNOW FLAKES TASTE THE SAME.

Don't own a pet
you can fit into a handbag.

If obliged to throw a punch,
don't tuck your thumb into your fist.

Try not to be the most
casually *dressed at a party*
unless you are the hostess.

Don't sleep with your bra on. So I've been told.

There's no rule that says girls can't mow the lawn.

Be precise with your praise.

YOU CAN START LATE,
LOOK DIFFERENT,
BE UNCERTAIN,
AND STILL SUCCEED.

Misty Copeland

Don't HEART your i's.

You don't get to DECIDE if
you are being funny.

You don't need to do
anything to prove you
like him. EVER.

If you cover yourself
with labels, be prepared for
people to put one on you.

There are plenty of tricks
to staying young. One is
matching pajamas.

Help your dad out on the computer. There's nothing he enjoys more than learning something from you.

LISTEN.

Try writing down your goals and your dreams. They should be the same.

STAND UP for your sister. And not just the one you're related to.

You're never too old
for fancy dress.

There's always time for
a milk shake.

The best is yet to come.

Essential Reading for Girls

❑ *Pippi Longstocking* . . . . Astrid Lindgren
❑ *I Capture the Castle* .Dodie Smith
❑ *Matilda* . . . . Roald Dahl
❑ *The Diary of a Young Girl* . . . . .Anne Frank
❑ *Anne of Green Gables* . . . . Lucy Maud Montgomery
❑ *The Secret Garden* . . . . Frances Hodgson Burnett
❑ *Little Women* . . . . Louisa May Alcott
❑ *When Hitler Stole Pink Rabbit* . . . . .Judith Kerr
❑ *Are You There God? It's Me, Margaret* . . . . . . Judy Blume
❑ *The Greengage Summer* . . . . Rumer Godden
❑ *Rebecca* . . . . .Daphne du Maurier
❑ *A Wrinkle in Time* . . . . .Madeleine L'Engle
❑ *Harry Potter and the Philosopher's Stone* . . . J.K. Rowling
❑ *The Color Purple* . . . . .Alice Walker

- ❏ *And Then There Were None*............ Agatha Christie
- ❏ *Charlotte's Web*...........................E.B. White
- ❏ *Emma*.................................. Jane Austen
- ❏ *How To Be a Woman*................... Caitlin Moran
- ❏ *The Handmaid's Tale* .... Margaret Atwood
- ❏ *To Kill a Mockingbird* .... Harper Lee
- ❏ *The Talented Mr. Ripley* ....Patricia Highsmith
- ❏ *Anne of Green Gables*...............L.M. Montgomery
- ❏ *White Teeth*...........................Zadie Smith
- ❏ *I Know Why the Caged Bird Sings*........ Maya Angelou
- ❏ *The Goldfinch* .... Donna Tartt
- ❏ *Ballet Shoes* .... Noel Streatfeild

Required Listening

- ❏ 'Embraceable You' . . . . Billie Holiday
- ❏ 'Me & Mr Jones' . . . . Amy Winehouse
- ❏ 'Stupid Girl' . . . . Garbage
- ❏ 'Fever' . . . . Peggy Lee
- ❏ 'You Don't Own Me' . . . . Lesley Gore
- ❏ 'Then He Kissed Me' . . . . The Crystals
- ❏ 'Don't Rain on My Parade' . . . . Barbra Streisand
- ❏ 'Shutter' . . . . Elastica
- ❏ 'You Don't Have to Say You Love Me' . . Dusty Springfield
- ❏ 'These Boots Are Made for Walkin'' . . . . Nancy Sinatra
- ❏ 'Master Hunter' . . . . Laura Marling
- ❏ 'Think' . . . . Aretha Franklin
- ❏ 'By Your Side' . . . . Sade
- ❏ 'Cry Baby' . . . . Janis Joplin

- [ ] 'Jolene'. . . . . Dolly Parton
- [ ] 'Gloria' . . . . Patti Smith
- [ ] 'One Way or Another' . . . . Blondie
- [ ] 'Bad Reputation' . . . . .Joan Jett
- [ ] 'Go Your Own Way' . . . . .Fleetwood Mac
- [ ] 'Woman'. . . . . Neneh Cherry
- [ ] 'I Wanna Dance with Somebody' . . . . .Whitney Houston
- [ ] 'You've Got the Love'. . . . . .Florence & The Machine
- [ ] 'Deadbeat Club'. . . . . .The B-52s
- [ ] 'Like a Prayer' . . . . Madonna
- [ ] 'Goldfinger' . . . . Shirley Bassey
- [ ] 'I'll Stand by You'. . . . . The Pretenders
- [ ] 'It's oh so Quiet'. . . . . .Björk
- [ ] 'You're So Vain' . . . . .Carly Simon
- [ ] 'Feeling Good' . . . . Nina Simone
- [ ] 'Doo Wop (That Thing)' . . . . Lauryn Hill
- [ ] 'Single Ladies'. . . . . Beyoncé
- [ ] 'You Belong with Me'. . . . . Taylor Swift
- [ ] 'Born This Way' . . . . Lady Gaga
- [ ] 'Lonely Daze'. . . . . .Kate Tempest
- [ ] 'Young Girls'. . . . . PINS
- [ ] 'Pedestrian at Best' . . . . .Courtney Barnett

Acknowledgments

I am very grateful to the following people who helped make this book possible: Laura Hanifin, a splendid photo researcher; Karen Gerwin, my friend and editor; my representative, Brian DeFiore; B. J. Berti and the entire staff at St. Martin's Press. And I am also thankful for the daily inspiration and support I receive from some pretty cool and talented ladies in my life, including Annie Lou Berman, Katherine McMillan, Amy Hutchens Wells, Kristin and Allie Meyer, my sister, Lizzy McMurtrie, my mom, Betsy Lamond, and most especially my wife, Colleen, who still laughs at my jokes.

PHOTO CREDITS